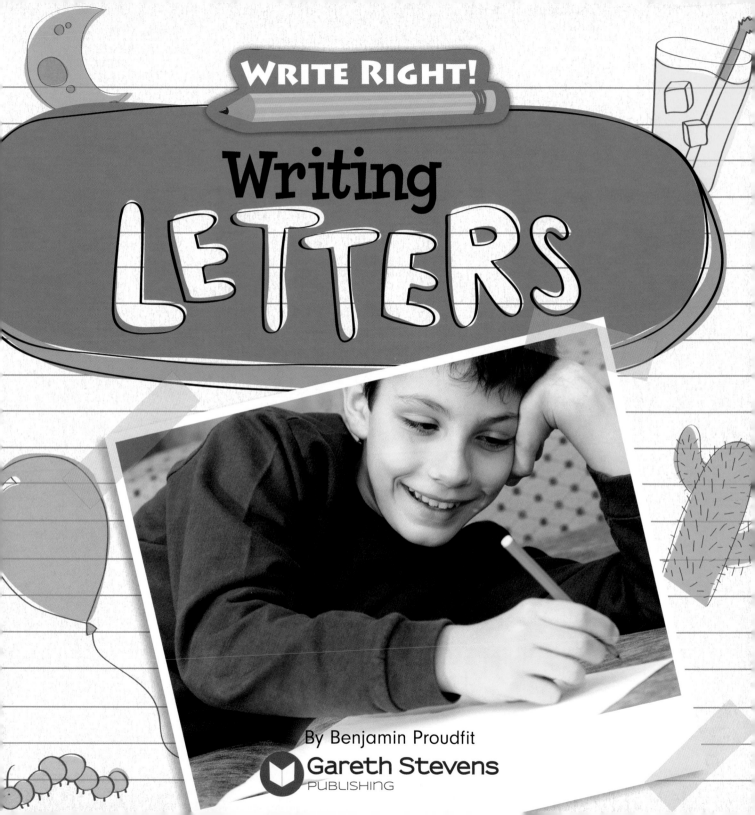

Write Right!

Writing LETTERS

By Benjamin Proudfit

Gareth Stevens
PUBLISHING

Please visit our website, www.garethstevens.com. For a free color catalog of all our high-quality books, call toll free 1-800-542-2595 or fax 1-877-542-2596.

Library of Congress Cataloging-in-Publication Data

Proudfit, Benjamin.
Writing letters / by Benjamin Proudfit.
p. cm. — (Write right!)
Includes index.
ISBN 978-1-4824-1133-1 (pbk.)
ISBN 978-1-4824-1134-8 (6-pack)
ISBN 978-1-4824-1132-4 (library binding)
1. Letter writing — Juvenile literature. 2. Interpersonal communication — Juvenile literature. 3. English language — Juvenile literature. I. Title.
PE1483.P76 2015
808.6—d23

First Edition

Published in 2015 by
Gareth Stevens Publishing
111 East 14th Street, Suite 349
New York, NY 10003

Copyright © 2015 Gareth Stevens Publishing

Designer: Sarah Liddell
Editor: Kristen Rajczak

Photo credits: Cover, p. 1 Hemera/Thinkstock.com; p. 5 © iStockphoto.com/Juanmonino; p. 7 Worytko Pawel/Shutterstock.com; p. 9 slava17/Shutterstock.com; p. 11 shironosov/iStock/Thinkstock.com; p. 13 Jack Hollingsworth/Photodisc/Thinkstock.com; p. 15 Fred Sweet/Shutterstock.com; p. 17 Ruggiero Scardigno/Shutterstock.com; p. 19 Andy Crawford/Thinkstock.com; p. 21 (background) mexrix/ Shutterstock.com; p. 21 (girl) Zurijeta/Shutterstock.com.

Printed in the United States of America

CPSIA compliance information: Batch #CS15GS: For further information contact Gareth Stevens, New York, New York at 1-800-542-2595.

CONTENTS

Words in the glossary appear in **bold** type the first time they are used in the text.

DEAR FRIEND...

Imagine a friend of yours has moved away. You both like to write and want to keep in touch even though you live far apart. You could write each other letters! Though there are quicker ways to **communicate**, writing a letter allows you to put more thought into what you're saying.

Like many types of writing, there's a certain way letters are set up, or formatted. The format and **tone** of a letter depend on whom you're writing to and what the letter says.

One good reason to write a letter to your friend is that you might get one back. It's exciting to get something in the mail!

TYPES OF LETTERS

There are many types of letters. The one you write to your friend who moved away would be a friendly letter. Friendly letters are commonly written to someone you know, such as your grandma. They might be used to give some news or just to say hello!

Business letters are more **formal**. They're often written to someone you don't know. You may use a business letter to ask for **information** or **complain** about something. Some thank-you letters will be written like a business letter, too.

ON THE WRITE TRACK

Have you ever had a pen pal? That's a person you may not know but exchange letters with. Some people are pen pals for many years!

You will likely choose slightly different words when writing friendly letters than business letters. Word choice helps set the letter's tone.

THE HEADING

Business letters should always have a heading with your address in the top right corner with the date under it. Your **recipient's** address is written under yours, but on the left side.

Friendly letters sometimes have your address written in the top right corner. This is a good idea if your recipient doesn't already have your address. Include the date, too. This lets the recipient know when you wrote the letter, in case you asked for a reply by a certain date.

ON THE WRITE TRACK

Letters can get lost in the mail. Putting a date on your letter lets the recipient know that. This can be important if you were trying to reach someone by a certain date, such as when sending an invitation.

James Reiser
312 Elm Street
Kansas City, MO 64101

March 20, 2014

Danielle Cruise
9112 Ridge Road
Springfield, MO 65801

9

PLEASED TO GREET YOU

You're probably most familiar with beginning your letter with "dear," such as "Dear Grandma." You can also start friendly, informal letters simply with "Hello" or "Hi." This is called the greeting. It's commonly followed by the name of the person you're writing to, but it doesn't have to be.

Business letters have different greetings. If you don't know the recipient's name, you can start with "Dear Sir or Madam." Another greeting for someone you don't know could be "To Whom It May Concern."

ON THE WRITE TRACK

A comma always follows the greeting in a friendly letter. A colon (:) follows the greeting in a business letter.

Letters may start simply with a person's name followed by a comma.

THE BODY

The main part of a letter is called the body. Skip a line after the greeting, and begin writing your first **paragraph**.

In a letter to a friend, the body might include news about your soccer team's latest game and ask if they are playing any sports. The body of a letter to your aunt might thank her for a gift she sent you.

The body of a business letter may ask a company for information about where to find a toy you want.

ON THE WRITE TRACK

Like any piece of writing, you should use an outline to plan out the body of a letter. An outline is a list of all the things you want to write in the order you'll write them, so you don't forget anything!

Show that a new paragraph is starting in your letter by **indenting** the first line. Or you can skip a line between it and the last paragraph you wrote.

SIGNING OFF

Once you've finished the body of your letter, write a short concluding statement, such as "I'll talk to you soon," or "Thank you for your time." This way, the reader knows the letter is coming to an end. Then, skip a line and get ready to close your letter.

You'd most likely use "Sincerely" to close a business letter. In a friendly letter, there are many ways to close, including "Love," "Yours Truly," and "Your Friend." Your signature follows the closing.

ON THE WRITE TRACK

When typing a business letter, write your closing and then skip several lines. Type your full name. Once you print out the letter, sign between the closing and the typed name.

When writing a letter or signing your name, use your best handwriting so others can read it.

Sincerely,

Rebecca Johnson

Rebecca Johnson

READ AND REVISE

After you've written your letter, read it over. Make sure it says what you want it to. If you notice any errors, sentences that could be clearer, or words you'd like to change, take time to **revise**. Check for:

- a comma between the date and year, such as in April 15, 2014

- a comma following the greeting and the closing, or a colon following the greeting in a business letter

- sentences always ending with a period (.), question mark (?), or exclamation point (!)

- sentences always beginning with a capital letter

- a complete heading

ON THE WRITE TRACK

Sometimes, you'll write a letter for school. Then it's especially important to revise! Read over the directions given by your teacher to be sure you've done all you need to.

Danica Moore
202 Harrison Street
Syracuse, NY 13210

sender's address

June 30, 2014

date

greeting

Dear Paula,

How are you? We haven't talked since you moved to St. Louis! I hope you like your new house.

Camp isn't as fun without you this summer. I was moved into the highest swimming group, though, and we get to compete with the camp across the lake. I'm really excited! Tamara is also swimming with me, but she doesn't dive as well as you do.

body

I think it would be fun to write letters to each other. My address, in case you already forgot, is at the top of this one.

Please write me back about your new city!

closing

Your Friend,

Danica

signature

17

WHERE'S IT GOING?

The final step of writing a letter is addressing the envelope. You need to put your name and address in the top left corner. This way, if the letter can't be delivered, it can come back to you.

Put the address of your recipient in the middle of the envelope. Make sure you use your best handwriting! Include the person's name on the first line and their street address on the second line. The third line should be the city and state they live in, followed by their **zip code**.

ON THE WRITE TRACK

You can use abbreviations, or shortened forms of words, when you write addresses. "ME" in the example stands for Maine. Check with a teacher or parent to make sure you've used the right abbreviation for the state you're sending the letter to.

Mary Thomas
456 Oak Tree Lane
Bangor, ME 04401

Jackson Corbit
1023 Swan Lakes Boulevard
Los Angeles, CA 91201

E-MAIL

E-mail is useful when you want to get a message or question to someone quickly. It's also an easy way to stay in touch.

"E-mail" is short for "electronic mail." When you write an e-mail, it should have a similar style and format to a letter, including a greeting, body, closing, and signature. Proper spelling and grammar should be used when writing an e-mail. This is especially important if you're writing to someone you'd like to **impress**, such as a teacher or politician.

ON THE WRITE TRACK

The signature in an e-mail could be a picture of your signature! Most often it's just your name, typed at the end.

LETTER IDEAS

Here are some ideas to practice your letter writing!

→ Write your mom or dad a thank-you letter for something nice they did for you.

→ Write to someone you admire and ask him or her about how they accomplished what they did.

→ Write to a relative who knows a lot about your family history and ask about it.

→ Write to your congressperson about an issue you're interested in, such as recycling.

→ Write a letter responding to something you read in the newspaper.

GLOSSARY

communicate: to share thoughts or feelings by sound, movement, or writing

complain: to express unhappiness

formal: following an established form. Also, having a tone of respect.

impress: to gain another's interest

indent: to move in from the edge of a piece of paper before writing a new line. Indents often signal new paragraphs.

information: knowledge obtained from study or observation

paragraph: a group of sentences having to do with one idea or topic

recipient: someone who receives something

revise: to make changes

tone: the general feeling of a piece of writing

zip code: a set of five or nine numbers added to an address to help sort mail

FOR MORE INFORMATION

BOOKS

Fogarty, Mignon. *Grammar Girl Presents the Ultimate Writing Guide for Students*. New York, NY: Henry Holt and Company, 2011.

Murray, Kara. *Simple and Compound Sentences*. New York, NY: PowerKids Press, 2014.

WEBSITES

Learn How to Write a Letter
www.funenglishgames.com/writinggames/letters.html
Practice writing a letter in this game.

Sample Friendly Letter
www.letterwritingguide.com/samplefriendlyletter.htm
Read this example of a friendly letter to review how to set up and write a letter.

INDEX